WHERE DO I BELONG?

WHERE DO I BELONG by Jayne Baumeister
Copyright © 2023 by Jayne Baumeister
All Rights Reserved.
ISBN: 978-1-59755-744-3

Published by: ADVANTAGE BOOKS™, Orlando, FL
                www.advbookstore.com

Library of Congress Catalog Information	
Name:	Baumeister, Jayne, Author
Title:	***WHERE DO I BELONG***
	Jayne Baumeister
	Advantage Books, 2023
Identifiers:	ISBN Paperback: 978159757443
Subjects:	Children's Books: Animals
	Children's Books: Action and Adventure
	Children's Books: Literature & Fiction
Keywords:	childrens Illustrated; best illustrated childrens books; childrens illustrated books; illustrated childrens stories

First Printing: August 2023
23 24 25 26 27 28   10 9 8 7 6 5 4 3 2

WHERE DO I BELONG?

WRITTEN AND ILLUSTRATED BY
JAYNE BAUMEISTER

There once was a dog named Mac.
He was a German Shepherd.

Mac dreamed about leading the hounds to catch some foxes. Mac always thought that he was a hound.

All the other hounds always barked at him. Mac said to Sam, who was the lead gray hound, "Some day I will show you that I'm faster than the other hounds!"

Tim, the owner of Mac, said to his friends, "Lets see if Mac can run faster than the other hounds."
Tim began blowing his horn and all the other hounds ran and started barking.

Mac started to run and he passed Stan, Sam and all the other hounds. Tim shouted, "Look at my dog Mac, he thinks he is a hound!"

All the other hounds started barking and the guys started laughing. Tim said, "Mac is a German Shepherd not a hound!" Mac heard Tim his owner laughing.

"Oh no," said Mac, " even my owner is laughing at me!" Mac ran as fast as he could, far away from the other hounds. Mac wanted to find where he belongs.

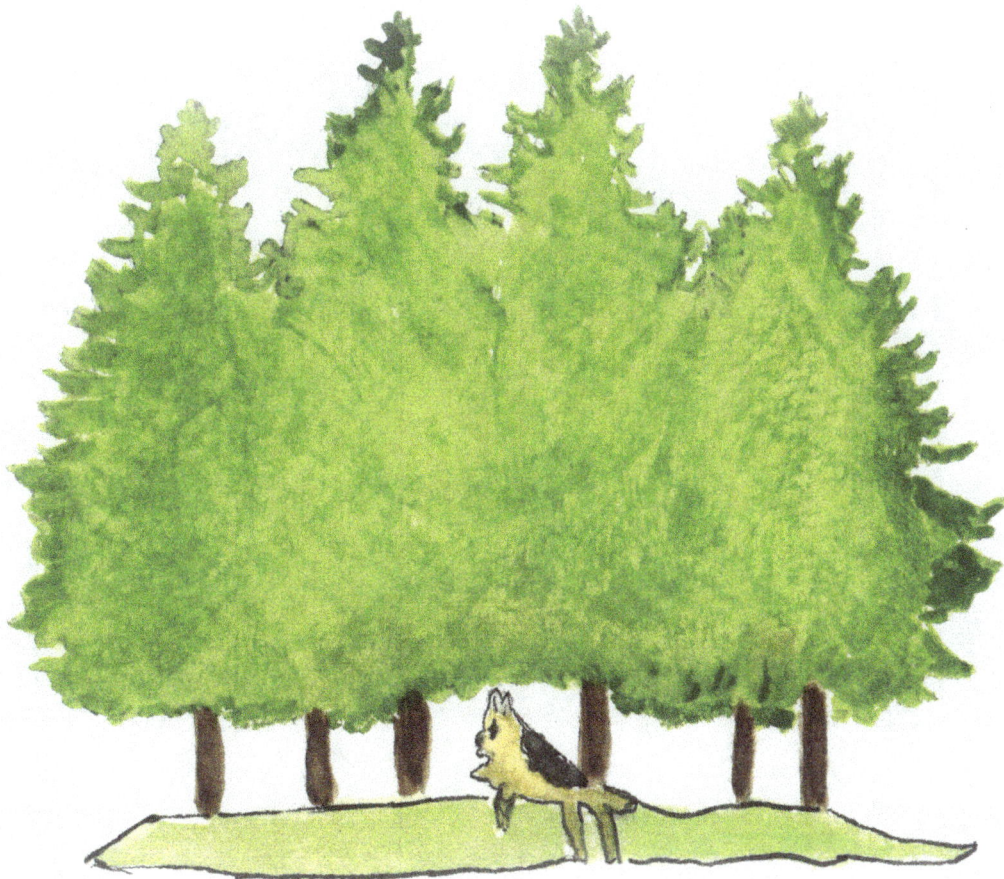

Mac came to a farm that has a horse. He came up to the horse and said, "hi my name is Mac, do you know where I belong?"

The horse said, "Neigh, neigh, my name is Buttercup and I am a horse." "I carry my owner, jump, run and I eat hay."

Then Mac said, "Oh no, I wouldn't want to be a horse and eat hay!" So Mac ran away.

Next, he met a cow and said, "hi my name is Mac." "Do you know where I belong?"

The cow said, "Moo Moo, my name is Bella and I am a cow. I make milk for my owner and I eat hay."

Then Mac said, "Oh no, I wouldn't want to be a cow and eat hay!" So Mac ran away...

Next he met a pig and said, "hi my name is Mac." "Do you know where I belong?"

The pig said, "Oink Oink my name is Piggy Wiggy and am a pig.
I roll around in the mud and I eat slop!"

Then Mac said, "Oh no I wouldn't want to be a pig and eat slop!" So Mac ran away.

Next he met a sheep and said, "hi my name is Mac." "Do you know where I belong?"

The sheep said, "Ba Ba my name is Penny and I am a sheep." "My owner uses my wool to make blankets and I eat grass."

Mac said, "Oh no, where do
I belong?" Mac began to cry.

All of a sudden Mac saw a little boy throwing a ball for his dog. He was running and barking and was trying to catch the ball.

Mac came up to the dog and said, "hi my name is Mac." "Do you know where I belong?"

"I am a hound," said Mac. And the dog said, "Woof, Woof, my name is Bailey the German Shepherd, and you are a German Shepherd too!"

Bailey said, "follow me, I want to show you something!"
Bailey and Mac ran all the way to the river.
Bailey said, "look in the water and you will see your reflection."
"See Mac, you look just like me!"

Mac said, "does that mean we chase Penny the sheep?"
Mac started barking.
"That's right," said Bailey

Mac was so excited, then Mac said, "I must go home and tell Tim my owner that I am a German Shepherd, not a hound!"

Mac ran and ran. He ran for hours and days... and finally he got home.

Mac ran in the barn and started barking and barking. Mac woke up Sam and Stan, and they started barking too.

"Oh yeah," said Stan, "this is Mac the German Shepherd who thinks he is a hound!"

Mac started barking and said, "I am a German Shepherd, not a hound. I chase balls and run after sheep."

Mac said, "I need to tell my owner Tim that I am a German Shepherd, not a hound!"

Mac ran into the house barking and said, "I am a German Shepherd and I chase sheep!"

Mac curled up next to the fire and sighed, " I am a German Shepherd, I finally found where I belong!"

For more information contact the publisher at info@advbooks.com

_A_dvantage
BOOKS

Longwood, Florida, USA
we bring dreams to life™
www.advbookstore.com